1,000

STRONG

VERBS

for fiction writers

VALERIE HOWARD

CONTENTS

INTRODUCTION

Are you searching for stronger verbs for your works of fiction?

Aren't we all?

A weak verb is one that's overused, only conveys a shallow meaning, and doesn't bring a powerful image to the mind's eye. The problem is, the weak verbs are usually the ones that pop into our minds first.

A strong verb, on the other hand, is a verb that performs three functions:

1. It names the action.

2. It tells *how* the action is performed.

3. It brings up an instant mental image.

For example:

"Walk" is a weak verb.

Sally walked across the room.

Meh.

Sometimes we add adverbs to prop up the verb and kind of help it along. This is a key indication that something is amiss:

Sally walked hurriedly across the room.

More descriptive, but a bit cumbersome. Let's use a strong verb in place of "walked hurriedly."

Sally scurried across the room.

See the difference? *Feel* the difference? In the first example, we understand that Sally got from one side of the room to the other, but that's all. We have no hint about Sally's emotional state as she walked. In the second example, we understand she walked in a hurried way, but it was a bit too explanatory and awkward. In the last example, "scurried" indicates a frantic hurry, and perhaps a little timidity with a mouse-like quality. We have a better picture of what's happening in the scene by changing one word in the sentence.

Here are a few more examples:

Weak: *Harry lightly touched the edge of the book.*

Stronger: *Harry trailed his fingers along the edge of the book.*

Weak: *Karen ran as quickly as she could to her closet.*

Stronger: *Karen charged her closet in a panic.*

Weak: *Lucy hit her palm on the desk.*

Stronger: *Lucy smacked her palm on the desk.*

Ready to weed out the weak verbs and not-so-helpful adverbs in your writing and replace them with strong verbs?

Okay, then, let's go!

(P.S. I've left some space at the end of this book for you to add your own favorite strong verbs as well.)

ASK

Gently

> Question
> Request

Urgently

> Beg
> Implore

Forcefully

> Cross-examine
> Grill
> Interrogate
> Pump
> Quiz

Attack

With Surprise

    Ambush
    Blitz
    Bombard

To do Harm

    Assail
    Assault

To Take Over

    Besiege
    Invade

Hurriedly

    Charge
    Rush
    Storm

BEND

Slightly

Angle
Arc
Arch
Buckle
Coil
Crook
Curl
Curve
Flex
Warp

Down

Bow
Crouch
Curtsy
Hunch
Kneel
Stoop

Bite

Daintily

Nibble

Continually

Chew
Gnash
Gnaw
Munch

Forcefully

Chomp
Crunch

Quickly

Nip

BOTHER

Slightly

Annoy
Bug
Irk
Irritate
Miff
Nettle

Moderately

Aggravate
Chafe
Harass
Peeve
Perturb
Pester
Rile
Ruffle

Severely

Exasperate
Madden
Plague
Vex

BREAK

In Tiny Pieces

> Crumble
> Crush
> Granulate
> Grind
> Mash
> Powder
> Shatter
> Smash

In Large Pieces

> Crack
> Fracture
> Fragment
> Snap
> Splinter

Beyond Repair

> Atomize
> Cripple
> Disintegrate
> Mangle
> Pulverize
> Ruin

Spoil
Wreck

Explosively

Burst
Bust
Obliterate
Pop
Rupture

Pieces Off

Chip
Flake
Peel
Scale
Shed

Down

Flatten
Level

Illegally

Deface
Vandalize

BREATHE

With Difficulty

> Gasp
> Heave
> Rasp
> Suck
> Wheeze

In Annoyance

> Huff
> Sniff
> Snort

In Short Burst

> Blow
> Puff

Obstructed

> Asphyxiate
> Choke
> Smother
> Suffocate

CARRY

A Heavy Load

> Heft
> Lug
> Schlep

Behind

> Drag
> Haul

A Distance

> Tow
> Trawl

In Something

> Cart
> Tote

CHANGE

Slightly

Adjust
Alter
Amend
Deviate
Diverge
Tweak

Largely

Reshape
Transform

For the Better

Modify
Refine
Revise

Specifically

Customize
Tailor

CLOSE

Quickly

Slam

To Keep In/Out

Bar
Bolt
Fasten
Lock
Seal
Secure
Shutter

Confuse

Mildly

    Muddle
    Puzzle

Moderately

    Jumble
    Perplex
    Stump

Severely

    Baffle
    Bewilder
    Confound
    Mystify

Purposefully

    Bamboozle
    Dupe
    Hoodwink
    Snooker

COVER

Partially

    Mask
    Screen
    Shield
    Shroud
    Veil

Completely

    Cloak
    Conceal
    Eclipse

CRY

Immaturely

Mope
Pout
Sulk

Softly

Choke up
Fuss
Sniffle
Snivel
Whimper
Whine

Loudly

Bawl
Blubber
Boo-hoo
Break down
Lament
Moan
Sob
Squall
Wail
Weep

Gut-Wrenching

Bemoan
Bewail
Grieve
Mourn
Pine for

CUT

Slightly

Clip
Incise
Lacerate
Nick
Scour
Slit
Snip
Trim

Into pieces

Chop
Dice
Divide
Halve
Mince
Quarter
Shred
Slice
Split

Down to size

Crop
Mow
Pare down
Prune
Shave
Shear

Violently

Carve
Cleave
Gash
Hack
Lop
Sever
Slash

DIG

Up

Exhume
Mine
Unearth

Down

Burrow
Delve
Drill
Tunnel

Out

Disembowel
Dredge
Gouge
Gut
Hollow out
Scoop

Through

Hoe
Sift
Till

DRAW BACK

In Surprise

> Flinch
> Recoil

In Fear

> Cower
> Cringe
> Shrink

In Pain

> Wince

DRINK

Daintily

Sip

Noisily

Slurp

Greedily

Drain
Guzzle
Knock back
Swill

EAT

Greedily

Chow down
Cram
Gobble
Gorge
Gulp
Nosh
Polish off
Wolf

A Large Amount

Feast
Overindulge

A Small Amount

Munch
Nibble
Snack
Taste

At a Table

> Dine
> Lunch
> Sup

Hesitantly

> Choke down
> Peck at
> Pick at

EMBRACE

In Fabric

>Bundle
>Swaddle
>Swathe
>Wrap

All the Way Around

>Confine
>Encircle
>Encompass
>Envelop
>Hem in
>Ring

Lovingly

>Cuddle
>Nestle
>Snuggle

FALL

Off a High Place

Cascade
Descend
Plummet
Plunge

Over

Overturn
Unseat

Down

Belly-flop
Drop
Flop
Keel
Swoon

Accidentally

Pitch
Topple
Totter
Tumble

FIGHT

Verbally

Argue
Bicker
Clash
Nit-pick
Quarrel
Quibble
Squabble

Physically

Brawl
Grapple
Scuffle
Skirmish
Struggle
Tussle
Wrangle
Wrestle

FILL

Overly

> Choke
> Clog
> Congest
> Crowd

An Object

> Load
> Pack

Forcefully

> Cram
> Stuff

Fix

Doctor
Mend
Patch
Remedy
Repair
Restore

Fly

Easily

> Glide
> Soar
> Float
> Wing

In One Place

> Hover
> Levitate

Quickly

> Jet
> Swoop
> Nosedive

GIVE

Grudgingly

> Fork over
> Shell out

To Many People

> Dispense

Charitably

> Bestow
> Contribute
> Donate
> Provide

Officially

> Award
> Deliver
> Present

GIVE UP

Willingly

>Acquiesce
>Cave
>Comply
>Defer
>Submit
>Yield

In Defeat

>Relent
>Relinquish
>Resign
>Surrender

HANG

On Something

Affix
Drape
Pin

In Midair

Dangle
Suspend

HIT

Accidentally

Bump
Collide
Crash

With a Sting

Cuff
Slap
Smack
Spank

Weakly

Bat
Bop
Rap
Swat
Tag

With Intention to Damage

Belt
Bludgeon
Clobber
Clout

Pulverize
Punch
Ram
Sideswipe
Slam
Slug
Smite
Sock
Strike
Tan
Thump
Uppercut
Wallop

Continually

Buffet
Pound
Pummel
Whale on

With Object

Cane
Flog
Lash
Paddle
Scourge
Switch
Whip

HURT

Continually

>Torment
>Torture

Mildly

>Mistreat

Moderately

>Afflict
>Bruise
>Punish
>Throttle

Severely

>Crucify
>Persecute
>Strangle

Permanently

Corrupt
Damage
Destroy
Poison

JUMP

A Long Distance

>Bound
>Leap

A Short Distance

>Hop
>Skip

Suddenly

>Flinch
>Quail
>Spring
>Start

Over Something

>Clear
>Hurdle
>Surmount
>Vault

Toward Something

Lunge

On Something

Pounce

LAUGH

Quietly

> Chuckle
> Titter

Loudly

> Bellow
> Chortle
> Guffaw
> Hoot
> Howl
> Roar
> Whoop

Daintily

> Giggle
> Tee-hee

Scornfully

> Cackle
> Crow
> Jeer
> Mock
> Snicker

Snigger
Taunt

LIE

Mildly

Distort
Fabricate
Fib
Fudge

Moderately

Deceive
Falsify
Misrepresent

Severely

Con
Perjure

LIFT

With Effort

       Heave
       Hoist
       Jack up

Easily

       Boost
       Elevate
       Hike up
       Raise

LOOK

Quickly

Glance
Glimpse
Scan
Skim
Spot

Subtly

Peek
Peer
Scout
Spy

Obviously

Gape
Gawk
Ogle
Stare
Watch

Continually

Admire
Appraise
Behold

Focus
Gaze
Observe
Peruse
Pore over
Regard
Study
View

Curiously

Examine
Explore
Eyeball
Gander
Inspect
Rubberneck
Scrutinize
Snoop
Squint
Survey

Hatefully

Glare
Glower
Lower
Scowl
Snarl
Sneer

MAKE NOISE

Short Sounds

Buzz
Ding
Ping
Whiz

Continual Sounds

Drone
Echo
Hum
Whir

Melodic Sounds

Chime
Knell
Peal
Toll
Trill
Warble

Airy Sounds

Swish
Whoosh

Technology Sounds

Beep
Blip
Chirp

Metallic Sounds

Clang
Clank
Rattle

Loud Sounds

Blare
Blast
Honk
Toot

Quiet Sounds

Creak
Jangle
Purr
Rustle
Tinkle

MESS UP

Mildly

>Blunder
>Mishandle
>Mismanage
>Slip up

Moderately

>Bungle
>Flub
>Goof
>Mar

Severely

>Botch
>Mangle

MOVE

Painfully

> Contort
> Writhe

Erratically

> Gyrate
> Hover
> Jiggle
> Waggle
> Wiggle
> Worm
> Wriggle

Nervously

> Fidget
> Squirm

Frantically

> Flail
> Thrash

Suddenly

Jerk
Twitch
Whisk

Daintily

Flit
Flutter
Frolic
Prance
Romp

Effortlessly

Float
Glide
Skate
Skim
Waft

PUSH

Gently

Elbow
Nudge
Press
Prod
Shoulder

Harshly

Bulldoze
Butt
Jam
Jostle
Muscle
Propel
Shove
Thrust

Together

Merge

PUT

Gently

> Deposit
> Insert
> Lay
> Place
> Rest
> Set

In a Specific Place

> Center
> Park
> Situate

Forcefully

> Drop
> Plop
> Plunk

QUIET/CALM

Assuage
Diffuse
Hush
Mollify
Muzzle
Pacify
Quell
Subdue
Tranquilize
Wane

Reach

Elongate
Lengthen
Protract
Span
Stretch

Run

High Speed

Bound
Dart
Dash
Fly
Gallop
Speed
Sprint

Low Speed

Hasten
Hurry
Hustle
Jog

At Something

Charge

Away from Something

Bolt
Escape
Flee
Zig-zag

In a Group

Race
Scatter
Stampede

Run (Liquid)

Slow Speed

Bubble
Dribble
Drip
Drizzle
Drool
Ooze
Plop
Pool
Puddle
Seep
Slop
Sprinkle
Trickle
Well

Moderate Speed

Slobber
Slosh
Splash
Spout
Squirt
Stream
Swamp

High Speed

Gush
Jet
Spray
Surge

SCRATCH

Mildly

>Score
>Scrape
>Scuff

Moderately

>Gash
>Scar

Severely

>Claw
>Gouge

SHAKE

With Fear or Cold

Palpitate
Pulsate
Quake
Quiver
Shiver
Shudder
Tremble
Tremor
Vibrate

With Imbalance

Flutter
Oscillate
Rock
Seesaw
Waver
Wobble

Violently

Convulse
Jounce
Rattle

SHINE

Momentarily

Flare
Flash
Flicker
Glare
Glint
Glisten
Glitter
Shimmer
Spark
Sparkle
Strobe
Twinkle

Constantly

Beam
Blaze
Flame
Gleam
Glow

SIT

Suddenly

    Collapse
    Plop down

Prolonged

    Perch
    Roost

Calmly

    Lounge
    Recline
    Sprawl

Uncomfortably

    Squat
    Straddle

Speak/Talk

Humbly

>Beg
>Beseech
>Implore

With Authority

>Advertise
>Announce
>Broadcast
>Command
>Enunciate
>Gloat
>Herald
>Lecture
>Lord over
>Preach
>Proclaim

To Alter Outcome

>Cajole
>Challenge
>Coax
>Coerce
>Complain

Correct
Egg on
Goad
Grouse
Inspire
Nag
Prod
Spur
Wheedle

With Difficulty

Falter
Garble
Hem
Mumble
Mutter
Slur
Spit out
Splutter
Sputter
Stammer
Stutter

Gently

Articulate
Utter
Whisper

Harshly

Admonish
Badger
Bark
Berate
Chasten
Chastise
Growl
Harass
Heckle
Henpeck
Hiss
Rant
Rebuke
Reproach
Reprove
Revile
Scold
Torment
Upbraid

Musically

Croon
Hum
Sing
Warble
Yodel

Continually

Babble
Chatter
Gab
Gossip
Jabber
Prattle
Yak

To Someone Far Away

Beckon
Invite
Summon

SQUEEZE

Gently

Compress
Constrict
Knead
Press
Squish
Wring

Harshly

Crush
Squash

STAB

Mildly

> Perforate
> Poke through
> Prick

Moderately

> Jab
> Knife
> Pierce
> Puncture

Severely

> Gore
> Impale
> Lance
> Plunge
> Run through
> Spear

STIR

Gently

     Blend
     Churn
     Mingle
     Mix

Quickly

     Beat
     Whip

STOP

Momentarily

Block
Defer
Delay
Freeze
Hinder
Pause
Postpone
Restrain
Squelch
Stall
Stymie
Suppress
Suspend

Permanently

Cease
Foil
Kill
Quash
Squash
Terminate
Thwart

Suddenly

Arrest
Halt

Partway

Bridle
Curb
Impede
Limit
Obstruct

Strengthen

Beef up
Bolster
Brace
Buttress
Fortify
Intensify
Secure
Shore up
Steel

Surprise

Mildly

Startle
Stun

Moderately

Amaze
Daze

Severely

Astonish
Astound
Bowl over
Dumbfound
Flabbergast
Floor
Numb
Paralyze
Shock
Stupefy

SWELL

Balloon
Billow
Blossom
Bulge
Burgeon
Flower
Inflate
Mushroom
Protrude
Puff
Pump

TAKE

Quickly

Bag
Jerk
Nab
Net
Pluck
Snag
Snap up
Snatch
Yank

To Keep/Store

Acquire
Amass
Capture
Clasp
Clutch
Collect
Glean
Grab
Grasp
Grip
Harvest
Hoard
Obtain

Reap
Reserve
Seize
Squirrel away
Stash
Stock
Stow

Wrongly

Pilfer
Pocket
Swipe

THINK

Deeply

Conceive
Concentrate
Consider
Contemplate
Deliberate
Meditate
Ponder
Reflect

Creatively

Envision
Fantasize
Imagine
Picture
Visualize

To Draw a Conclusion

Analyze
Assume
Calculate
Compute
Deduce
Estimate

Evaluate
Gather
Gauge
Infer
Presume
Reason
Reckon
Speculate
Suppose
Surmise
Theorize

Too Much

Fixate
Obsess

THROW

Gently

Cast
Flick
Flip
Sling
Toss

Violently

Chuck
Fling
Heave
Hurl
Pitch

THROW AWAY

Banish
Discard
Ditch
Dump
Eject
Eliminate
Expel
Jettison
Junk
Reject
Scrap
Trash

TIE

Loosely

Fasten
Interlace
Lace
Lash
Strap

Tightly

Bind
Cinch
Knot
Secure
Sew
Stitch
Suture
Tether
Truss

TILT

Slightly

Angle
Incline
Slant
Tip

Upside down

Capsize
Overturn
Upend

TOUCH

Barely

> Glance
> Graze
> Kiss
> Skim
> Trace
> Trail

Thoroughly

> Fondle
> Handle

Aggressively

> Grope
> Jab
> Paw

Curiously

> Finger
> Poke
> Probe
> Prod

Gently

Brush
Massage
Palm
Rub
Stroke
Tap

Lovingly

Caress
Pat
Pet

Nervously

Fiddle with

TURN

Partway

Hinge
Pivot
Screw
Shift
Swivel
Twist

Suddenly

Dodge
Spin
Swerve
Twirl
Veer
Wheel around

Slowly

Crank
Wind

In Circles

Corkscrew
Revolve
Rotate

WALK

Quickly

Scamper
Scoot
Scramble
Scurry
Scutter
Trot

Slowly

Dawdle
Lumber
Plod
Shuffle
Slog
Traipse
Trudge

Quietly

Pad
Slide
Slip

Loudly/Heavily

Stamp
Stomp
Tramp
Trample

Aimlessly

Amble
Drift
Meander
Mosey
Pace
Ramble
Roam
Stray
Wander

With Confidence

March
Parade
Sashay
Saunter
Stride
Strut
Swagger

Leisurely

Advance
Range
Rove
Stroll

With Difficulty

Careen
Falter
Lurch
Reel
Stagger
Stumble
Sway
Teeter
Toddle
Totter
Trip
Waddle
Weave

Stealthily

Creep
Lurk
Prowl
Shadow
Skulk
Slink

Slither
Sneak
Tiptoe
Trail

Timidly

Edge
Inch
Sidle

Through Something

Wade

WANT

Mildly

>Desire
>Fancy

Moderately

>Hunger
>Thirst

Severely

>Covet
>Crave
>Lust

WEAKEN

Abate
Decrease
Diminish
Ease
Ebb
Fade
Recede
Stifle
Wane

WORK

Drudge
Labor
Slave
Strain
Strive
Struggle
Toil

WORRY

Mildly

>Disquiet
>Unnerve

Moderately

>Brood
>Fret
>Overburden
>Stew
>Stress

Severely

>Agitate
>Agonize

WRINKLE

Slightly

>Crease
>Crimp
>Pucker

Severely

>Crinkle
>Crumple

WRITE

Hastily

>Doodle
>Jot
>Scratch
>Scrawl
>Scribble

Deliberately

>Compose
>Draft
>Inscribe
>Pen
>Print
>Record
>Type

YELL

Low Tones

Boom
Holler
Thunder
Trumpet

Shrill Tones

Caterwaul
Screech
Shriek
Squawk

Long Tones

Bay
Howl
Wail
Yowl

Short Tones

Bark
Yelp
Yip

Happy Tones

Cheer

OTHER STRONG VERBS

Alarm
Blanch
Boot
Buff
Cluster
Congregate
Crab
Dally
Dazzle
Drench
Electrify
Elicit
Evoke
Extract
Fester
Fizzle
Flap
Flaunt
Flock
Flounder
Froth
Gag
Gargle
Grate
Grouch
Gurgle
Ignite

Jolt
Jut
Muster
Nuzzle
Pave
Percolate
Pledge
Pose
Punt
Radiate
Razz
Reek
Ricochet
Roast
Salivate
Saturate
Scrimp
Simmer
Slander
Smear
Snare
Snuffle
Soak
Splay
Spurt
Strip
Strum
Swarm
Swelter
Swindle
Tax

Thrill
Thrum
Tug
Validate
Vaporize
Wallow
Wax
Wrench

About

VALERIE HOWARD has been a self-published author since 2011. She's a follower of Jesus, the wife of a pastor, the mother and teacher of two energetic boys, a graduate of Bible college, and the author of several novels, plays, non-fiction books, and children's books.

If you liked this book, you may also like:

1,000 Character Reactions from Head to Toe
1,000 Helpful Adjectives for Fiction Writers

(Both free with Kindle Unlimited.)

Get a free book at ForIndieAuthors.com

www.Facebook.com/forindieauthors

www.Instagram.com/forindieauthors

Made in the USA
Monee, IL
21 August 2022

12111338R00066